"In all, several thousand people took part over fourteen years…
They worked a ten-hour day, six days a week, and they were all
men — with the sole exception of Emily Roebling."

David McCullough, *Brave Companions*

Big thanks to Tom Richardson for his technical expertise and to
Dr. Bill Wishinsky for his thoughtful comments. FW

Published in 2019 by Groundwood Books / House of Anansi Press
groundwoodbooks.com
Second printing 2023

We gratefully acknowledge for their financial support of our publishing
program the Canada Council for the Arts, the Ontario Arts Council and the
Government of Canada.

Canada Council   Conseil des Arts
for the Arts   du Canada

ONTARIO ARTS COUNCIL
CONSEIL DES ARTS DE L'ONTARIO
an Ontario government agency
un organisme du gouvernement de l'Ontario

With the participation of the Government of Canada
Avec la participation du gouvernement du Canada | Canadä

Library and Archives Canada Cataloguing in Publication
Wishinsky, Frieda, author
How Emily saved the bridge / Frieda Wishinsky ; illustrated
by Natalie Nelson.
Issued in print and electronic formats.
ISBN 978-1-77306-104-7 (hardcover). — ISBN 978-1-77306-105-4 (PDF)
1. Roebling, Emily Warren, 1843-1903 — Juvenile literature.
2. Brooklyn Bridge (New York, N.Y.) — Biography — Juvenile literature.
3. Bridges — New York (State) — New York — Design and construction —
Biography — Juvenile literature. 4. Brooklyn Bridge (New York, N.Y.) —
History — Juvenile literature. I. Nelson, Natalie, illustrator II. Title.
TG25.N53W57 2019   j624.2'3092   C2018-903674-5
C2018-903675-3

The illustrations were created with digital collage and found photographs.
Design by Michael Solomon
Printed and bound in China

FSC
www.fsc.org
MIX
Paper | Supporting
responsible forestry
FSC® C144853

For my extraordinary editor,
publisher and friend Sheila Barry
(1963-2017), whose insight and
warmth made working on books a joy.
I miss you, Sheila.
And with many thanks to wonderful
Nan Froman for her wise words and
understanding.
FW

For Mary Anne and Margaret.
NN

HOW EMILY SAVED the BRIDGE

The Story of EMILY WARREN ROEBLING and the Building
of the Brooklyn Bridge

FRIEDA WISHINSKY

PICTURES BY
NATALIE NELSON

Groundwood Books
House of Anansi Press
Toronto / Berkeley

THE BUILDERS OF THE BRIDGE
DEDICATED TO THE MEMORY OF
EMILY WARREN ROEBLING
1843 - 1903
WHOSE FAITH AND COURAGE HELPED HER STRICKEN HUSBAND
COL. WASHINGTON A. ROEBLING. C.E.
1837 - 1926
COMPLETE THE CONSTRUCTION OF THIS BRIDGE
FROM THE PLANS OF HIS FATHER
JOHN A. ROEBLING. C.E.
1806 - 1869
WHO GAVE HIS LIFE TO THE BRIDGE

"BACK OF EVERY GREAT WORK WE CAN FIND
THE SELF-SACRIFICING DEVOTION OF A WOMAN"

THIS TABLET ERECTED 1951 BY
THE BROOKLYN ENGINEERS CLUB
WITH FUNDS RAISED BY POPULAR SUBSCRIPTION

"Emily Roebling inspired me to become an engineer, Nate. She helped build this magnificent bridge."

"Wow! How did she do that?"

"Come on! I'll tell you her story on our way to Brooklyn."

$$2x + 5 = 25$$
$$x = ?$$

When Emily Warren was growing up in Cold
Spring, New York, in the 1850s, many girls were
told they weren't smart, especially in math or
science. Few women went to university. Women
couldn't vote, own property or sign a contract.

But Emily loved science and math.

She wanted a good education.

She wanted to learn all she could.

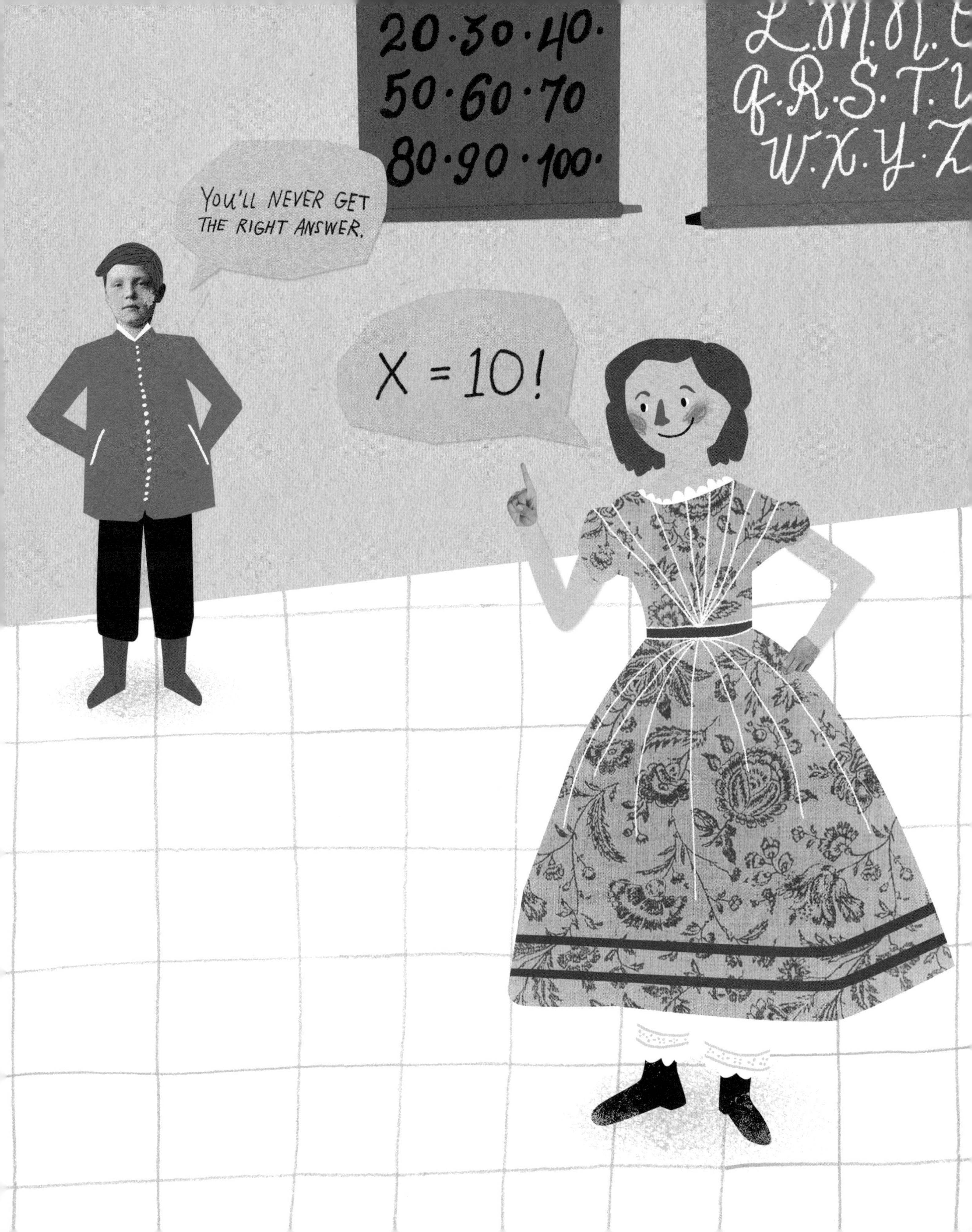
20·30·40·
50·60·70
80·90·100·
YOU'LL NEVER GET THE RIGHT ANSWER.
X = 10!

Emily's older brother, Gouverneur Kemble (or
G.K. for short), believed in her.

When Emily was fifteen, he enrolled her at the
Georgetown Visitation Convent in Washington, DC,
where she studied many subjects, including botany,
algebra, history, French and geography. She earned
high honors.

During the American Civil War, G.K. became a general. In 1864, when Emily was twenty, she visited him at his military camp and met his aide, Washington Roebling. Washington was a soldier, an engineer and a bridge builder. He was also the son of John Roebling, a famous bridge builder.

Washington thought Emily was wonderful.

He bought her an engagement ring six weeks after they met.

Emily and Washington were married on
January 18, 1865. Soon after, Washington helped
his father build a bridge across the Ohio River.

In 1867, Washington's father began working on
a bigger and more challenging project — a bridge
that would span New York's mighty East River
and connect Manhattan and Brooklyn. Until then,
the main way to cross the river was by ferry. When
it was foggy or the river froze, ferries were often
delayed. Sometimes they even got stuck in the ice.

I CAN'T SEE ANYTHING IN THIS FOG.

The new bridge would be a suspension bridge. Like many suspension bridges, its two tall towers would be built on top of caissons — giant, bottomless, timber-and-metal boxes, floated into position then sunk to the bottom of the river.

Four main suspension cables made of steel-wire ropes would be strung between the towers to support the roadway deck.

But on June 28, 1869, as John Roebling stood on a beam surveying the bridge site, a ferry jammed against the dock and crushed his foot. He died less than a month later from an infection.

Who could take over his job? Washington, of course! But the bridge was such a big, complicated project. How could he build it without his father?

Emily encouraged her husband to take on the project.

Washington agreed to build the bridge.

The work began.

Soon the caissons were filled with compressed air to keep river water from rushing in. Men climbed down ladders through a series of airlocks — passageways with airtight doors — to dig into the riverbed. As the towers rose higher and higher, the weight sank the caissons further into the soft mud until they reached bedrock.

But digging with hand tools like picks and shovels was exhausting. Breathing the hot, heavy, foul air was almost unbearable.

Some workers developed a painful and dangerous illness called "caisson disease," or "the bends." It was caused by moving too quickly from the compressed air inside the caissons to the normal air pressure at the river's surface.

Many people who worked on the bridge, including Washington, developed this terrible disease.

PLEASE BE CAREFUL, WASHINGTON.

Despite being ill, Washington kept working and supervising. He tried to prevent floods, fires and explosions, but accidents still happened.

When a candle tipped over inside one of the caissons in 1870, Washington rushed down to help and rescue his men.

And then one day, in late 1872, Washington became so sick that he couldn't walk or stand.

Emily ran her home, nursed her sick husband and took care of their son, John.

She also kept records, read books, consulted daily with Washington and learned everything she could about bridges and engineering. She even met with manufacturers and explained how to design parts for the bridge.

And every week, sometimes two or three times a day, Emily trekked over to the bridge site, spoke to the workers and monitored the construction. At first, some of the men didn't believe she knew much about bridges or engineering. But she explained every aspect of the project so clearly that soon many believed *she* was the chief engineer.

Washington never returned to the bridge again.

By 1873, the digging had been completed and the caissons were filled with concrete to support the towers.

Soon the two huge towers rose high above the river. The four main suspension cables were strung from anchor blocks on each shore up over the towers. Vertical suspender cables were then hung from the main cables down to the roadway deck.

The cables, designed and made by the Roebling company, were strong, but in 1876 the committee in charge of funding the bridge decided to buy some steel cable wire from the J. Lloyd Haigh Company.

Washington and Emily were shocked and dismayed, and in 1878, when one of the Haigh wires snapped, it was clear that Haigh had sold them shoddy wire!

Washington wouldn't take any chances. He added extra strands of good wire to strengthen the cables.

Haigh eventually went bankrupt, and he was later sent to Sing Sing prison for writing bad checks.

For a time during construction, a wood footbridge stretched high over the towers. A special pass was needed to take this risky trek above the East River. Because of the danger, the footbridge was completely closed to the public just months after it opened.

In 1881, a walkway was placed over the bridge's new steel floor beams, extending from one city to the other. On a windy December day, Emily led a small group, including the mayors of New York and Brooklyn, across its narrow wooden planks.

When the group reached the other side, they toasted Emily and the bridge with champagne.

DON'T LOOK DOWN.

HOW FAR TO THE END?

GULP.

SAFE FOR ONLY 25 MEN AT ONE TIME. DO NOT WALK CLOSE TOGETHER. NOR RUN. JUMP. OR TROT. BREAK STEP!

W.A. Roebling. Eng'r in Chief

Finally, in 1883, after fourteen difficult years, the bridge was ready to be opened to the public.

It towered over the East River. It was beautiful and strong.

Emily Warren Roebling was the first to cross the completed bridge. She carried a live white rooster as a symbol of victory and good luck.

When her carriage passed, the bridge workers tipped their hats and cheered.

SHE SAVED OUR BRIDGE.

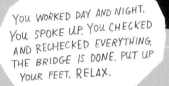

After the bridge was built, Emily fixed up a new house, traveled to Russia and England, helped soldiers returning from the Spanish-American War and became active in promoting women's rights.

But that wasn't all.

Emily wanted to become a lawyer. In the 1890s, women rarely studied law, but that didn't stop Emily.

In 1899, she graduated in law from New York University. She was fifty-six years old. Her final essay focused on equal rights for women.

I'M OFF TO LAW SCHOOL.
OUTRAGEOUS!
IT'S NOT LADYLIKE TO ARGUE.
IT'S LADYLIKE TO HAVE DREAMS AND WORK HARD. THAT'S WHAT I'VE DONE. THAT'S WHAT I'LL ALWAYS DO.

"The name of Mrs. Emily Warren Roebling
will thus be inseparably associated with all
that is admirable in human nature, and with
all that is wonderful in the constructive
world of art."

Congressman Abram S. Hewitt
at the dedication ceremony for
the bridge, 1883

SIX AMAZING FACTS ABOUT the BROOKLYN BRIDGE

1. First of Its Kind The Brooklyn Bridge was the first steel-wire suspension bridge ever constructed. John Roebling proclaimed that steel was the metal of the future.

2. Celebration On May 24, 1883, New York threw a big party to celebrate the opening of the bridge. President Chester A. Arthur, Governor Grover Cleveland and many dignitaries attended, along with Emily Roebling. Brooklyn and Manhattan declared a holiday. A band played and fireworks lit up the sky. At the stroke of midnight, the bridge was opened, and more than 150,000 people streamed across in twenty-four hours.

3. Disaster A week after the official opening, disaster struck. A rumor that the bridge was about to collapse sparked panic, and people rushed to get off. Twelve people died and thirty-six were injured in the crush.

4. Elephants on the Bridge? To convince people that the bridge was safe after the disaster, showman P. T. Barnum was hired. In May 1884, he arranged to have twenty-one elephants march across the bridge. The bridge and the elephants survived the crossing.

6. Still Standing Tall The bridge still stands today, more than 135 years from the day it was completed. Thousands of people from all over the world cross it every day.

5. Skyscrapers The majestic bridge towers rose higher than any other structure in New York at the time. They were the city's first skyscrapers.

FOR FURTHER READING

Books for Young Readers
Curlee, Lynn. *Brooklyn Bridge*. New York: Atheneum, 2001.
Mann, Elizabeth. *The Brooklyn Bridge*. New York: Mikaya Press, 1996.
Ratliff, Tom, illustrated by Mark Bergin, *You Wouldn't Want to Work on the Brooklyn Bridge!: An Enormous Project That Seemed Impossible.* New York: Scholastic, 2009.
Zaunders, Bo, illustrated by Roxie Munro. *Gargoyles, Girders and Glass Houses: Magnificent Master Builders*. New York: Dutton, 2004.

Selected Sources
Books
McCullough, David. *Brave Companions: Portraits in History*. New York: Simon and Schuster, 1992.
McCullough, David. *The Great Bridge: The Epic Story of the Building of the Brooklyn Bridge*. New York: Simon and Schuster, 1972.
Wagner, Erica. *Chief Engineer: Washington Roebling, the Man Who Built the Brooklyn Bridge*. New York: Bloomsbury, 2017.

Articles
Brady, Sean. "Brooklyn Bridge Construction: Overcoming the Odds." *Engineers Journal*, 2015. Online
Griggs, Frank. "Brooklyn Bridge, Part 2." *STRUCTURE*, November 2016. Online
McNamara, Robert. "The Brooklyn Bridge Construction in Vintage Images." *ThoughtCo.*, November 3, 2017. Online.

Source Notes
1 "In all…Roebling." David McCullough, *Brave Companions.* New York: Simon and Schuster, 1992, p. 46.
31 "The name of … world of art." *Address delivered by Abram S. Hewitt on the occasion of the opening of the New York and Brooklyn Bridge, May 24th, 1883*. New York: John Polhemus, printer, 1883, p.12. Internet Archive. Online.
The photos in the collage illustrations are from images in the public domain.

NOTE

The main text of *How Emily Saved the Bridge* is based on research. The speech balloon conversations are imagined. The art, likewise, has been created in an imaginative spirit, with a nod to illustrated newspapers from the time that the bridge was built.